OTHER SAINTS ARE AVAILABLE

Mark Fiddes' first collection, *The Rainbow Factory* was published by Templar Poetry in 2016 following the success of his award-winning pamphlet *The Chelsea Flower Show Massacre*. He is a winner of the Oxford Brookes University International Prize and the Ruskin Prize. He was placed third in the UK National Poetry Competition and was a runner up in both the Robert Graves Prize and the Bridport Prize. His work has been published in *Poetry Review, POEM, The New European, The Irish Times, Magma, Aesthetica* and *London Magazine* among many other journals.

First Published in 2021
By Live Canon Poetry Ltd
www.livecanon.co.uk

All rights reserved

© Mark Fiddes 2021

978-1-909703-50-6

Thanks

Margaret Mary Theresa Fiddes (1933-2018) who only saw a few of these poems. As a mother, teacher and gardener, she did growth better than anyone. 'Secateurs' is all about her.

My family. Maribel, Alec and Sergi have had a lot to put up with. Thank you. Every day you amaze me. My sister Clare who's still making Mum proud. My father Chris whose painting and lyric intuition remains an inspiration.

The poets of the Middle East, particularly Zeina Hashem Beck, who has been a beacon for voices from around the region. All the other poets who have kept each other going between lockdowns and despots: Geraldine Clarkson, Rishi Dastidar, Sasha Dugdale, Katie Griffiths, Eleanor Hooker, Tom D'Evelyn, Tara Skurtu, Kostya Tsolakis, Tania Hershman, Thomas McCarthy, Josephine Corcoran, Alexander Velky, Tessa Foley and a hundred more.

Finally, my wonderful publisher Helen Eastman and her team at Live Canon for the countless ways they innovate and energise live poetry.

Contents

POLITE SAFETY NOTICE

Somewhere near you, a man in late middle age will be sitting on a bench
with his head on fire like a safety match.
On buses and trains, other men will smolder suddenly roaring into flame
from the neck up. I'd be surprised if you haven't seen them.
They would cry out but without mouths, their teeth grind away inside their faces.
Do not approach them. Like eucalyptus in forest fires, they burn
too fiercely to be extinguished, black oil pumping from a fossil heart,
their limbs so wickery and feet already stone.
It's too late to intervene. You must step away. Let Nature take its course.

Somewhere near you, a much younger man will be gripping a school desk,
as his life rockets into the void.
His brains will spill over the mocking examination paper then slop down
into the Victorian sewer system of which we are still so proud.
All he has ever learned is what's expected of him. Show no comfort.
No doors out. No path back. No window except his peeping phone.
What quivered with joy now pushes up his gullet like a great white swan of pain.
It's too late to intervene. You must step away. Let Nature take its course.

Somewhere near you, the men in between will be wearing rubber flippers
running a marathon over razor blades carrying babies.
They'll do anything for attention.
Others barricade themselves inside and watch furiously through sand bags
or cling to flagpoles or bury themselves alive in golden man pits.
Value your sympathy. Don't waste it. This was all hard-wired from the start.
Never is power more toxic than when it is almost spent.
Come back in 100 years. None of this can be saved.
It's too late to intervene. You must step away. Let Nature take its course.

EL PACTO DEL OLVIDO

We walk the canal under plane trees,
words in one pocket, silence in the other
past palettes stacked for *la cooperativa*,
the air thick with dust and late harvest.
We talk of work, cards we've been dealt,
the missing people, our grown children,
whose absences now lengthen beside us.

I explain how this hour a lifetime ago,
Nationalists executed the men too unfit
to march to the "work camps" in France,
leaving the bodies somewhere over there
to rot, dropped like sacks in familiar dirt.
They thought nothing could be quieter
than a country of unmarked graves.

Once in step, we speak of nothing more.
Someone's taking pot shots at the rabbits.
Swallows speed type through pylon wires.
An irrigation ditch fills, a tractor stutters.
Black damsons clack against dry mouths.
Homewards we scrape, shale underfoot.
Peace grants us time and bitter fruit.

SECATEURS

Back in my mother's garden,
the fences were always broken
as the whole of creation clambered in
with tendrils and buried nests
and shanks of love-lies-bleeding.
Star-bright stock, always night-scented,
lit the crazy paving to a fern bank,
where toads with golden eyes
guarded my marijuana crop disaster.
Ivy followed us indoors
with moths that slept in lampshades.
Beetles fell from our homework.
Chrysalides glistened in sock drawers.
Lawns and borders were outlawed
being too needy and English.
Any frost chose its victims sparingly.
Every Spring tasted of honey,
long before the arrival of bees.
Geraniums thrust through rubble
so green was the blade of her knife.
Everything grew back stronger
the harder it was cut.
In her hands, life was inevitable
until her fingers grasped only ours
over the bedrail. She coughed
then turned her back once more.

GOLDFINCHES

Our tea cools down, the last from the pot.
Through the kitchen window we watch
two goldfinches pecking seed from a feeder.
Old storm clouds smoke along the tree line.
Everywhere else has floods, as firemen
rescue an incontinent island from itself.
They say another superbug is on its way.
Leather or rust has seeped into the room.
I can't see him
when he asks how he's done as a father.
I tell him
I haven't found the job description yet.
It's not the answer we are looking for.
A day will come when my dam wall cracks
and the finny words will slip through
but we need more apocalypse than this.
Instead, we riff on goldfinches.
How they mistake England for paradise.

PROXIMITY

A finger
on the blue in my wrist,
professionally touching
where the violets flow,
reading my heart
better than anyone.
Airborne antiseptics sing
of dry martinis.
Outside, we await results.
All of the gossip mags
have been trashed
for fear of infection.
For everything else
bothering mankind
they have a brochure.
Against public decrees
I rub my itchy eyes
when I see her fingers,
steepled like Durer's,
marbled with age,
a loose wedding band,
resting in her lap.
She squints for her name
on the doctor's board
as if to a foreign shoreline.
I want to settle my hands
on hers like a dove
or a son or prayer.
I need to tell her
that whatever it is,
we already have a cure.

REGARDING ANNE SEXTON

About the cigarette hammered between your fingers:
does it to nail you to the world?
I imagine you never puff where inhalations are available,
that you're always running out of matches.
The problem with this photo is, you're doing that look
like a thousand grainy poets before and after you.
Eyes left. Like you have just seen a burglar.
You're projecting more Joan than does you credit:
Crawford, Collins, Fontaine, Sutherland, d'Arc.
This might be fine if you were in the smoldering business
but I had you down as The Stepford Arsonist.
So there's not much in this shot I can believe in,
except that you are sitting on a metal filing cabinet
in a simple white dress fit for a prom or first communion
in front of a book stack that could crush a lumberjack
next to the Royal typewriter you called your "church"
ready, after the photographer has gone, for you to slip
inside again, so thin and high and wide-shouldered,
looking straight ahead at the task in hand.

PORTENTS AND FLARES

We drag sofas out into our back yards
to catch the meteor shower.

Glasses chink from a neighbour's garden.
They're listening to TV updates on the stars.
Given recent news, it's the perfect time
for a Messiah.

I sit with my arm around your shoulders.

I am full of flowers.
My mind is scented with crushed leaves.
It knows you are looking and cannot see.

Someone in Ireland has texted in a sighting
but here the clouds have stolen Orion's bow.

You are still thinking about the vase I broke
and why in a perfectly mechanical Cosmos,
even the asteroids are late.

You go back inside.
The Perseids never come.
Next door the fun swells into a party.
Castor turns up with Pollux and a big dog
as the night pours in, right up to the brim.

INVENTORY: BOOKS

When the removal men come, they use cotton gloves and masks for
the books.
"It's the dust," he shakes his head, like we were in Nagasaki instead
of Tooting.
Penguin classics, their black spines cracked with effort, slip in beside
Elmore Leonard.
It's Boll to Cocteau in the next carton and a dog-eared frottage of
existentialists.
Elsewhere, Middle Earth meets middle class. Narnian queens spoon
Truman Capote.
Carver should have his own box but he's joined by Tour Guides from
The Lonely Planet.
Aristotle, Hobbes and Locke nuzzle Jean Rhys smelling of church and
whisky bottles.
Thin, interesting pamphlets from the Poetry Book Fair jam between
Chekhov's women
and fifteen Oxford Histories that remain impregnable as Dame Vera's
bluebird cliffs.
All the damned verse cramps up in sizes so diverse they say it must be
flat-packed.
Then they're gone –ß in their tottering truck with the boxes stacked in
sugar cubes.
Off to storage with the rest of us for an uncatalogued period of sorting
shit out
while our dust still grips the empty shelves like finger marks left on
a window ledge.

THE KODACHROME BOOK OF THE DEAD

Frozen in their Kodaks,
our old folks wear slippers
to protect the carpet from their feet.

Colours leech. A tap drips.
Dinner lingers in another room.
A yucca erupts on the lawn.

The lounge is an orgy
of fakery: leatherette armchairs,
plaster dogs, silk orchids,

mock encyclopedias
and more fringe than necessary
on lamps, hairdos, lips, pelmets

plus random tassels
wherever there is dangling
and come-hither velvet.

If a grandparent smiles
it is like a wolf had stopped by
for tea and a slice of Battenberg.

Parents vogue in folky
knitwear surrounded by cigarettes
and the Sixties.

Is this how they will see us,
our early years tucked into albums
balanced on the knee like babies?

Will pages crackle as laminates
separate and we stare back red-eyed
as hounds from blind pubs?

Whereas our last few decades
will click past in seconds on a screen,
backlit, cropped and cherry-bright.

There they can find us,
between swipes, catching our breath,
wiping the joy from our sleeves.

AN EARLY SWIM

She cuts down her lane like scissors through blue silk
with barely a snip; her deft turn at each end is a stitch.
One morning, she will rise from the ladder, the pool
draped over her shoulders like a cape of kingfishers.

He rolls like a barrel of vintage port cast overboard,
his crawl Shakespearean in its comedy and slaughter
causing small weather events and tile grout erosion.
His breast stroke venerates a torso of many bosoms.

Together, they leave behind a fresh pigment in the air
brushing the bellies of low birds with aquamarine.
She cycles off, helmet first, into the budding day
while his car awaits, sore-eyed and smelling of dairy.

NEW BABEL

Vapours trail. Cranes pull heaven closer.
Construction crews arrive by the hundred
in patched buses; plastic Ganeshes dangle
between dainty curtains in the windscreen.
Overalled in dust, the workers cut a dash
with fusilier moustaches and tartan scarves,
all smoking, their hard hats at half-cock
as they saunter off through the earthworks
like a sunny day on the Somme.
Sixty floors up, coarse desert winds roar up
from The Empty Quarter through floors,
picture windows, mini-gyms, lift shafts
and other figments of luxury living.
A father of twins from Delhi finds balance
on a steel beam, hanging from a chain,
hooked on a spar, propped on a brace,
clipped to a gantry, gripped by a miracle.
In the world below, a super yacht slots
into the Marina, a pearl among pearls
set in turquoise as pleasure seekers wheel
earthwards on phosphorescent wings.
Five miles out in the Gulf, smoke spindles
from a second tanker that has taken a hit.

CORNOGRAPHY

to poet Geraldine Clarkson

If you have to tweet photos of cow parsley,
please include the crushed beer cans.
On those verges embroidered with poppies,
don't forget the fly-tipped mattress.
Show only streams strewn with Tesco trolleys
and valleys planted with wind crucifixes.
Depict the grey logistics depots along the M1.

Because now I live in a most desert-like state
where the sand has drawn a veil over the land.
A tubercular milk of concrete dust smothers us.
Before leaving for work, I stretch a damp cloth
over my mouth and nose, tie it with shoe laces
as the mini-market just sold out of face masks.
If the sun blinks open, you only see cataracts.

Here, your wheat pics sigh cornographically.
Your bosky grotto shots could get me deported.
Better if you find a cheap edition of John Clare,
press wildflowers between your favourite pages.
Let them suffocate beautifully and mail it to me
care of The Empty Quarter, Rub' al Khali.
I'll see what I can do with the seeds.

DAY OF THE ORYX

Dawn lifts from the desert city
first as vapour then as dirty flame.
Cranes stretch their canted necks.
Past Al Qudra, piledrivers restart
the hearts of luxury devlopments.

The land's great malls yawn open.
Machines swish the marble floors
like giant grey electric oysters.
Night security men haunt the exits
thinking about their next smoke.

Silica glitters on every balcony.
Across the shallows of fake lakes,
the waking dreams of expatriates
glide back from the jungles, woods,
foothills and steppes of childhood.

In a well-crimped palm avenue,
two gardeners in neon overalls
fork pinks into the steaming earth.
The Keralan boy pings his bike bell
then takes the long way round.

From the underpass they drift,
spirits of the dunes, white-bellied,
their horns tuned to the wind
under the melting frangipani trees
brushing the bougainvillea.

Past the security gates, they pause
at the grassy roundabout to graze,
to lap the dew of early sprinklers,
to watch the hot, fat man jogging
when eyes meet, athlete to athlete.

The gazelles all freeze and he slows
to a walk, already too late for work.
Over Frosties, he will tell his kids
the sand Bambis have moved back.
Today, he will be close to wizardry.

SELF PORTRAIT WITH THE STATE OF TEXAS

She returns at night in a flat-bed truck
stacked with scaffold and dangerous paints.
The canvas moon dips for a closer look.
Coyotes remember her from way back,
scampering like puppies in her tail lights.
Even the bones in the sand know Frida.
Her song wove the sinew that bound them.
Her brush, dusted with cactus magic,
planted their dreams into museums of art
to bloom as tea towels and fridge magnets.

The Wall approaches like a line of chalk
drawn across a board by a naughty child,
rising to a sheer cliff in her headlights,
white as the house in Washington, D.C.
where Eisenhower refused to meet her.
She butts the tailgate up to the concrete
and starts on the first of many parrots
in spectacles, quiffed like Leon Trotsky
bursting through a can-can feather sunset
that plumes into leaves and fat larvae.

Agave goddesses nurse earth babies.
Their breasts bleed the milk of lemon trees.
Monkeys toy with sugar skulls and crutches
around a volcano gushing Houston crude,
gardenias and jeweled hummingbirds.
Razor wire grows into a thorn necklace
ornamented with the pearls of search lights.
Here hang her hearts with festive arteries
that lace together a dozen Kahlos,
a thousand, a Frida nation looking askance.

By dawn, the desert's drawn ocean blue.
Drone patrols rise up with the vultures.
A Texas Ranger Facebooks his selfie
with Karl Marx, thinking it's Kenny Rogers.
When this goes viral, Fox News blows a fuse.
The President drains his lake of Whitewash
for the ultimate violation… but it's too late.
A billion Fridas have broken through
his wall into cyberspace, saving screens,
saving souls and everything in between.

OLFACTORY SETTINGS

The first symptom is loss of smell.
It has me cradling fruit like a miser,
piling it up in fragrant pyramids.
For last night's big balcony cheer,
I walked out with a Seville orange.
As they clapped and flashed phones,
I picked at its skin and kept sniffing.
The apartment's previous occupant,
an Austrian, left a cupboard stinking
of fish which I open like cheap wine.
I have fancy after-shaves on rotation
to keep the olfactory receptors alert.
Apothecary drops stain my pillow.
I switched from showers to baths,
lying for hours absorbed by labels
of photoshopped lavender and sage,
Prousting about in the white foam
in remembrance of the old ad slogan:
Things happen after a Badedas bath.
I hope not; this decade is already full.

FISHES OF VENICE

Once the waters turned Tiepolo blue
fishes returned to nibble the city's feet.
blooming around the piers of gondoliers,
as if the sea had remembered a birthday
and brought flowers to La Serenissima.
Antiquities grinned from the canal bed.
Desdemona weeds spread on sandy pillows.
Light played xylophones under bridges.
Crabs scuttled with bags between piazzas.
Dolphins filed back as if from a long war
followed by the mermen and merwomen,
propped up on elbows along the quays,
fanning their tails, boasting of plans
for submarine palaces in the new Republic.
Across the lagoon, moored in quarantine,
his gunwhales stuffed with silks and stories,
Marco Polo watched through tinted glass
how the sun as it blazed loved his city
as much as the ardent plague itself.

UNICORN JUICE

They had a nose for water, a sixth sense, being islanders
distantly related to storm clouds and the Kraken.
On their radios, shipping forecasts rocked them to sleep
sea-county by sea-county, named for battles, sand banks
and brave little islets jutting their chins out to sea.

"Nice day for it," they would say, meaning rain, not sex.
When their ditches began to fill and their bogs to spill,
they blamed mainlanders and those bewitched by science.
"Stiff upper lip," they said, meaning denial, not sex.
Few talked of the flies or the stench rising from the fields.

Babies started choking while the old folded like deckchairs.
"No one does methane better than us!" yelled the tabloids
as fresh excrement bobbed in and out of Parliament
and foamed through the microphones of talk shows.
"Take back control," they said, meaning fear, not sex.

With Union Jack gas masks, cakes and street parties,
they named 'The Great Defecation' a public holiday.
"How well this goes with carriages and tweed," they said,
bottling the flow through gutters with vintage stoppers
calling it Uncorn Juice, a product of Empire, not sex.

AFTER DELIUS

On the occasion of not leaving the European Community, March 29th, 2019

For an hour or two over breakfast
the lethal Etonians were hushed
on the day we meant to leave.
Common or garden birds threshed
a chorus from thin British hedges.
A bog-standard UK sun rose up
sixty non-decimal minutes before
Europe to shake off a bleary March.
Pigeons paraded along the gables
in regimental medal regalia.
New blossom reported for duty
bunting all the pissed-up alleys.
Not a chemist ran short of insulin
and the growling tide of lorries failed
to make a delta out of Kent.
Hate was too hungover to fry up
the Full English with trimmings
in saucy tabloids and talk radio.
On the day we meant to leave,
a bird of unsettled status flew in
to Devon from an African hot spot
laden with unregistered eggs
searching the lanes for spare nests
and any true love crying "cuckoo."

METAPHYSICAL WOMAN

For hours, I have studied how
you leave a print on the day
like a stamp of authenticity
or guarantee of life on earth.
Lipstick on the coffee cup's rim.
Vapour trails of bright nails
streaked across the stratosphere.
A dent in the orange peel
where your thumb has been.
How a depressed friend grips
onto your arm like a stair rail.
Why the town will greet you
as if it has been so long
when only a week has passed.
Your chair angled to the table
in a such a way the yappy dog,
the reversing rubbish truck,
the hurrying priest melt away.
One hair unwinds as a spring
around the loaded ashtray.
Even the storks are watching
from the top of the clock tower
to learn what to tell their eggs
about motion and rest.
The moment you fall asleep,
the gears of the world unmesh
like an earthquake in reverse.
Voices from the street below
ask hey what happened there?
Did you feel it too?

CARDIOGRAM TO A FRIEND

When you break your heart
it stays right where you broke it,
in the lay-by or motel room.
Mortified, it will change colour
to hide from further damage
as a litter bin or cheap sheets
or a wooden bench for lovers
to carve with their initials.
It will attract lichen and stains.
You will never see it again
with such infinite camouflage.
Meanwhile, a brand-new heart
will bud inside you, feeling
wobbly and delicate at first,
falling over too often, kittenish,
loving too much of anything
that has a pulse and risking
the whole world for a kindness.
This heart too you must prepare
to give up to an empty hallway,
as footsteps fade in late snow.

ULTRASOUND

Thanks for showing me the scan.
See, he has your spine;
a belt of stars with Pleiades fingers,
the Milky Way of his ribs,
his thumb docked into a lunar skull,
an umbilical cord for space walks.
You are his celestial spheres,
the only music he hears
for at least the next fifteen years.
I guess the father must be Zeus
for he is made of Gods and heroes.
Birth-side, he is already a legend,
your tiny Orion.
May his arrows find only monsters.
May his dogs run faithfully to heel.
May his great bears all be soft ones.

LOSING WINTER

Crows mob the alders with intent, then descend
to stab the sodden field and tear at hedgerows
newly flecked with buds and random daffodils.
They caw and swagger. The sparrows scatter.
A red kite swings by spying out collateral damage.
It's too early for them to lose their winter.

Aside from Hurricane Week which felled a tree,
we bore witness to one shy snowfall – that was all.
Frost turned up, glitter-balled the grass for a week
then glammed off East for some real climate action.
Even the mists appeared as drizzle in a grey cloak
before endless unattended matinees of rain.

Today's news shows twin lambs on shaky legs.
Americans dressed as pallbearers raise a groundhog
that online conspirators report may be a robot.
I'll wait. It's not over. Not until phone masts sing
with cocky swallows and our bodies itch with seed.

THE ROBOT DOGS GO WALKIES

The robot dogs are exercising in the park
among scampering autumn leaves.
Owners from the Faculty have them flip
backwards like chromium cheerleaders
then make them chase their antenna tails
to beg for non-existent biscuits.
In between, all the robot dogs stamp
as if they have an appointment elsewhere.
Their laser green eyes tell you nothing
except they have sufficient power
to maul a child or guide a blind man home.
Their robot grand-puppies have yet to pilot
a spacecraft to safer galaxies or shepherd
mankind off the edge of a cliff.
Maybe they're already planning a Masterdog
with a history in real estate and reality TV.
Now they whir politely back to Cybernetics
for five years' further Fintech funding.
A genuine cat watches from the laurels
framing a report back to ginger colleagues.
So many questions unanswered.
A few academics linger with plastic bags
to scoop up any artificial intelligence
that may have dropped onto the grass.

THE NINE DEGREES OF IRONING

Ayurvedic ironing treats
the whole trouser, not just the crease.
You are the steam, the fragrant clouds,
the gentle pressure on the lap.

Freudian ironing prevents
the recurrence of deep crenellations
around buttonholes and pockets
that will trigger thoughts of murder.

Catholic ironing demands
early and total submission to heat
on the assumption that reluctance
is sewn into every collar and cuff.

Tory ironing transfers
all credit to the owner of the iron,
and the supplier of the electricity.
If the set up fails, you're on your own

Feline ironing happens
when you are otherwise engaged.
With just their tongues they attend
to the draping of all domestic pleats.

Quantum ironing requires
that all shirts are chaotic by nature.
Smoothness is merely statistical.
You are the calm in their storm.

Drunk ironing succeeds
where all other ironing fails
except for the disappearance of single
items into the long sock of the night.

Marital ironing yearns
for a crumple-free partner only
when love lies puckered and unworn
at the back of your wardrobe.

Stoic ironing is pressing
your ninth cotton blouse, escaping
sweet vapours to a life as perfectly
wrinkled as last night's sheets.

IN THE BUSHES

The jungle bird does not do fireworks.
He sidles along the branch,
ordinary as a poet at a bus-stop, overcoated,
cap raffishly angled, a scarf stolen from a rainbow.
He plays skiffle on the bark until he gets to mate
whereupon he sings about it ceaselessly
like it was the first time it ever happened up tree.
"Get a life," say the sloths and bandicoots.
"We've all been there, or thereabouts."

MY LOCKDOWN QUIFF

Today I present as a Burnley defender from the 1970s.
I might as well grow sideburns and open a small pub
for when the good times roll again.
You make a fuss about cutting it, but I have watched you
with scissors and bacon making carbonara,
laughing like Ingrid Pitt in The Vampire Lovers.
Your barber's window would display all the heads of state,
poorly drawn in pencil as an enticement to passing males.
The Trumpen Helmet,
finely spun by evil fairies from chicken wings.
The Netanyahu Lid,
forged from gun metal and closed to everything.
The Boris Mop,
a pastoral English Merkel with scurf and privileges.
The Erdogan Shadow,
frail remains that still claim to be growing freely.
The Kim Jong Bun,
a black lacquer box of Pandora's surprises.
It's not a lack of trust in you but a fear of new dictators
popping out of my head, unstoppably,
requiring mustaches, parades and domesticated tigers.
A marbled palace of design atrocities might be necessary.
Our boundaries re-drawn, I'd put a tank on your lawn.
Yet tonight, your calming towel drapes my shoulders.
Your comb unknots my dread as your Ladyshave races
down the back of my neck with its electric lady teeth,
at electric lady speed with electric lady needs.
This will be a day we talk of many lockdowns from now,
when the cracks between tiles sprouted real human hair.

EVEN THEIR CATS HAVE TITLES

"MAKE WAY FOR THE POETS!"
bouncers bellow through the oyster bars
on a rhyming planet in a near multiverse.
Champagne flutes chink as the poets pass.
Fans chant their hit stanzas like anthems:
"Be kind while there is still ti-i-ime"
cheering the poets' fur-lined, silver-tipped
metaphors, their diamond punctuation,
their perfect skin and exquisite teeth.
Couturiers copy their specs and anoraks.
Perfumers catch their souls in ambergris.
Here, words are the only legal tender
in circulation, traded by page or mouth.
The more they mean, the more you buy.
Watch as legions of the beautiful throw
themselves on the poets who never tire
of adoration living in lofts of gold.
Even their cats are bestowed with titles
to sit in judgment on red satin pillows
over criminals and civil disputations
as the poets ride their latest swans
across the Thames and debate the state
of the comma in *The Chimerical Times*
or legislate like tigers on mescaline.
Bankers, meanwhile, scuff along the curb
to drafty parish halls for workshops
on liquidity ratios and credit swaps.
They share tips on banana bread and jam.
Lawyers ping pong in community centres.
Estate agents tend damp allotments.
In pissy underpasses, politicos spray paint
genitals and seed the coming revolution.

THE GREAT IMPERSONATOR

He could do almost anyone:
Tommy Cooper, Kenneth Williams
stuck up there above the mantelpiece
in his crown of real thorns.
Wounds. Big feet. INRI written
on the cross like it was a trade union
for light entertainers.
And a smile that knew the audience
was always on the edge of convulsion.
"It's the way I tell 'em," he'd say,
mimicking the great Frank Carson.
My grandmother had other crucifixes,
in the bathroom, in every bedroom,
even one in the airing cupboard,
but none were half as talented.
All this and a plaster Mary presiding
over the gas fire below
with her battery-operated heart aglow
in fondant robes, that skywards look
like she'd heard it all before.
When grandmother went, so did he
with the words of Ronald Reagan,
whispering urgently at the wake:
"Nancy! Nancy!"
He was never the best with names.

HOW TO APPROACH A FIELD OF SUNFLOWERS

The trick is to come up from behind
as melt water thunders
down the irrigation ditches
and the canal drops below rat holes.

Around you, the green has burst
from chlorophyll into opera,
clenching, sighing, swaying its big arse,
pimping everything it touches.

Trust the linnets,
slim with song and egg production,
to lead you along the orchard's edge
to face the sun. There you'll see them.

Tall with their backs to you.
like a field of Apostles,
their heads gently flaming.
We should have called them *fireflowers*.

Don't look any in the face.
You might come over all evangelical
and spend the rest of your life
painting yellow chairs with blue edges

THE FUTURE PERFECT TENSE

They will never have been so beautiful
as they are here by the pool taking selfies
on a stick in their wedding clothes together,
white tulle misting over blue water,
morning suit as faint as distant smoke
when the candy stripe golf cart edges into shot.
Years later they will have asked who's the man
with a gloved hand in pink plaid shorts?
Will he have been the secret agent dispatched
to the resort by one of the agencies of despair
with marital bed bombs and mortars of remorse
Or just another questing American
who's lost a ball and requires the clubhouse bar?
They will never have been so complete
as they are here by the pool taking selfies
on a stick in their wedding clothes together,
white mist, distant smoke, interrupted.
Couples many times more married gaze on,
slung up between palms in rattan hammocks
waiting for the cicadas and salted snacks.

LITTLE THUNDERS

I stand by the open window
following coastal lightning.
Your skin turns bone white
as you drank the only light
left to us before you slept.
Now you rise and you fall
with the *Marinada*, its salt
breath over the olive groves,
and stork-thatched towers,
over the moon-slack canal.
These blistered blinds belly
into the memory of my hands
that still hold the first kicks
of our sons' feet that beat
against your ocean drum.
Back then we all sang along
unaware we even had a tune.
The chorus was accidental,
stuck with band aids and jam
as we marched to the clatter
of spoons in far off storms.

I BELIEVE IN MIRACLES

The restaurant has long boiled over,
menus wiped, folded beside tills.
An anniversary candle still flickers.
I scribble the air for the bill.
Between the clams and the house white,
we forget the subplot of our bodies.
How our skin tells one story;
the hard proof marks of marriage
on stomach, brow, liver and thigh,
while our spirits *ad lib*
as if auditioning barefoot for anything.
An overgenerous tip,
despite the spelling mistake on the cake.
Ridiculously wrong coats at the door.
The obligatory argument
on the way home with flat-iron silence.
The surprising absence of rain.
The sigh of waking roses in the hallway.
The dimmer switch that needs fixing.
An exhibition of family and friends
on the mantelpiece and one embrace
before the empty fireplace.
Then the softly killing fingers of this,
our half-remembered song.
The last dance around the kitchen
negotiating the knives and pans
with the mortgage payments on hold.
Just our wonky, funky history on bass.

LIGHT ENTERTAINMENT

Stiff-backed in his chair, he waits
for the shadows behind the black bamboo
to come out for the evening.
Damp seeps from the slatted seat.
There will be owls and foxes shrieking like babies.
Flowers will be played by chimes and glockenspiels.
Twilight will grow more leaves.
Moths will peel from the moon.
Honeysuckle will croon all the forgotten tunes.
Ivy walls will sprout secret doors
to terraced kingdoms of cabbage, bean and rose.
He will catch her kitchen jostle, her furious kettle,
its gentle click.
She will find chamomile, biscuits and pillows
and a tall, dark Scottish detective
followed everywhere by murder and grudges
until sleep rests the Kindle on her knees.
He will go back inside, switch off all the lights
and lie in the ploughed furrow beside her
replaying the shooting star;
how you only need to see one,
for it to burst your night apart.

THE GREAT AMERICAN SONGBOOK

Just a few nights after the 9/11 attacks,
they dropped Rule Britannia
from the Last Night of the Proms.
As we watched the screen in Hyde Park
your star-spangled banner dripped
from our damp branches and we wept
stones to Barber's Adagio for Strings.
Slatkin's hands no longer conducted
bars of music but the space between,
fathomless and mute
while violins lifted us above the rain
and the wreckage of sodden picnics,
all breath suspended on one final chord
as if this too might be our last,
floating between faraway tenements,
down freeways, under sulking flyovers
over plains of native spirits and mist
to silver birches and shining shores.
Here, we were both smaller and greater
than ever before
becoming all of the work songs,
the slavery and the freedom songs,
the hobo and the crossroad songs,
the Motor City songs,
the protest and the Opry songs,
the love songs that made us possible.
Now gone.
Lost somewhere between Presidents,
as we wait once more
for Slatkin's hands to raise us,
to conduct the fathomless and the mute.

ONE WAY BACK TO BABYLON

"Can I go home yet?"
Such a small voice for a big statue

On a grey stool in the corner
a British Museum guard yawns
and turns away from the conversation.
Maybe this happens every day.

"Where's home?" I whisper.
"Where the sea kisses the sky,
where the shells have lost their voices."

A charioteer taps my shoulder.
"Me too. Have you come with horses
wild enough to drive us back to Hellas?
No one needs us here."

Across Room 115 they queue politely:
        a jade dragon,
        a gold l lama,
        a bronze king,
        a silk princess,
        a whale bone chessman,
        an ivory dildo,
        a granite Buddha
        whose smile has long since flown,
        the inevitable mummy
        an alabaster bishop,
        an ebony judge,

like I have the keys to a Magic Bus
to repatriate every exhibit to its ruin.

The British Museum guard excavates
a nostril and checks his watch.
There's still an age to pass before lunch.

OVERHEAD, A HELICOPTER

Limbs line the road from trees
chopped raw by the hurricane.
The sky adds crows.
"Didn't we send a gift?" I say
slowing behind an ambulance.
"I couldn't find the date," you say.
"It must have been after his op'."
Chainsaws duel around the corner.
Overhead, a helicopter.
"He's probably wandering around
in baggy pants with a catheter."
Brake lights pool in puddles.
At the turn, a Range Rover twists,
crushed and ribboned with tape.
A copper sips from his Starbucks,
waves us on like any Wednesday.
Sheep crowd the field's far triangle.
A man jogs the ridge with his dog.
An advert on the radio
sells us a deeper, cheesier pizza.
Without a cloud it starts to rain
like it's not Essex anymore
but a monsoon archipelago.
I switch my windscreen wipers on.
A mother and daughter tip toe
in matching anoraks from the back
of a different ambulance.
"Maybe we can catch his birthday?"
you say, like we've been practicing
calamities on our own for years.

ANOTHER SOLSTICE

With no virgins to sacrifice,
I spent this year's birthday in Tesco
freezer-deep in pimpled turkeys,
Bublé crooning *O Come All Ye Faithful*
and some spillage in aisle six.
Outside, as the grey day shriveled
westwards, I received a Firebird.

Its wings blazed across the horizon,
feathers dropping like molten gold
over tower blocks and commons.
Blinded vans pulled into the curb.
Everyone turned to capture my gift
on their phones before its flight back
to Eternity leaving ashes in our eyes.

8TH NOVEMBER, 2016

Something made us smaller today,
pushed under scudding bulletins.
TV polls predict a humbling.

You can already see the landslide
burying light behind the eyes
that sell us flat whites and pastries.

You can nose out the rot of hope
in burger bars and and betting shops
where we snack out on fat and luck.

Even the bus-stop tastes of Trump
here in my newly foreign land.
In other news they forecast snow.

We're just grateful for the blanket.

THE CORRECT USE OF SAINTS

In the crimson satin lobby
a quartet saws through Schubert
like angry Victorian dentists.
A breakfast separates you and I.
We wait for one of us to turn up
and jump start the weekend
with a word or sudden kindness.
You order poached. I'm fried.
A waiter buttoned like a hussar
brings us a German newspaper
on a staff, stiff with home affairs.
I suggest we see the Bruegels.
Enough of painting, you say.
I mention the famous tapestries.
You tell me I'm missing the point.

Drawn by the city's stone gravity
we drift down to the riverside,
to the bridge covered with chains
and bright padlocks left by lovers,
scratched with hearts and arrows.
A cruiser slips under the arches.
On deck, knots of tourists wave
to us as if we were somewhere
on the map like the city's saints
on plinths beside us in dark robes,
holding up their electric lamps
still flickering even in daylight.
You lever my hand from the rail,
asking if I still believe in miracles.
"What else is there?" I reply.
You must believe in something.

IN THE KING'S HEAD

She extends one hand to play the air like a pianist.
The other arm links with a fat man who threads her
gently from summer through the saloon bar doors.
She wears clothes the berry red of forest brambles.
Her fingers practice complex scales upon the light
that has trailed her into our lunchtime lager land.
They sit at a table laid out for diners and she smiles,
tilting her head upwards as if to catch a lost word
snagged among cherubs on the stucco ceiling.

Her palm seances the place mats and I am certain
everything is pure vibration and that she can hear
me now below her cloud, flapping and stuttering
like an early flying machine run on gas and rotors
as hope still snatches at wires and grinds the gears.
All this she assimilates as if this pub were nothing
more than a tuning fork; we the broken hammers.
They rise to leave. He too unclicks his white stick
before weaving her back to the hot metropolis.

THIS IS HOW IT WILL WORK

Tell us where it hurts, perched up on your ledge.
How the city turned you into a gargoyle,
a bent and concrete thing, rain running out your butt.
Tell us how you medicate. Think gyms, yoga and gin.
Maybe techno.
Your support network next. God, Netflix or therapy?
Salsa lessons are still popular.
We will then consult the wind and a twig,
the scattering of scat and the morse of frogs,
to wild you back a bit.
A typical introductory box may contain the following:
Wads of moss for stress, pressed to a crawling scalp.
Half a blackbird's shell for smashed spirits.
A spray of hawthorn berries for hardening of the heart.
A tray of water meadow left beside the pillow
for when you cry yourself to sleep.
A jay's wing when you're dull and fading.
An acorn to fight hopelessness (plant between cracks).
Wild cress for the bathtub if you're crushed and breathless.
Any questions, our customer services team is a call away.
This month they are sparrows.
Just don't expect a complete cure.
The city already claims you to its landfill memory.
Like mites and traffic noise, it will die with you in bed.

INFINITY AND HER FRIENDS

Even as blue
nested eggs, the starlings
must have shared their big secret
by speckling in code or morse between shells.
How else did they choreograph over frozen dykes
and fields such a wild and fluent heart that span though
its dark parabolas to express a love only bodies in motion
ever comprehend? At least that is how I recall it now
at rest on a slatted bench as brash parakeets peel away
from neatly boxed park trees too crazy green with
each other like teenagers on a shopping spree
with parental credit cards, mocking
whatever it is to flock, to knit
the quivering air into a
cloak thrown over
infinity.

ASSEMBLING GOD
(flatpack instructions)

Catalogue man kneels in a white room.
The slit in his drawn pecker-head smiles
but he's not happy at the sudden Arctic
filling up the frames in which he's stuck
in silence with crudely rendered tools.
Up next, a rough black cross says NO
to the screw-washer combination he grips.
He considers the best-selling Crucifix,
how it might have worked out differently
had Golgotha been planned by Ikea:
the Redeemer figure self-assembling,
slotting his cross-bar upside down,
thorns missing, the wrong size of nails,
starting from scratch, cheating with glue,
the Divine Intervention of Saint Velcro®
for the flapping midriff modesty panel,
all the time refusing to ask for help.
Would the big religions be more forgiving
with just a wordless instruction manual
and a chirpy call center south of Cork?
The drawn man stacks his planks and slats,
but cannot find the pictogram reference
for blow torch or small incendiary device.
Next door, another man is hammering
like it's Asgard: soon there will be drills,
meat balls and whelps of marital bliss.
The drawn man feels like a surplus shelf
as the world's top-selling book case
slides gracefully, infinitely, sideways.

MAN RAY vs DUCHAMP: A TRIPTYCH

Game 1. 1924
(Still from the film "Entr'acte by Rene Clair)

As the stunt men of fuckery, they face off between wars
astride a stone ledge over the rooftops of Paris.
The chess pieces on the board parade in the square below.
Duchamp is Black. Breezes stiffen the hair into a horn.
Man Ray is White, wearing a banker's striped suit.
His hand hovers. His resignation crashes like a horse
down onto pebble stones.

Game 2. 1952
(Photograph by Michel Sima)

Caught at the outbreak of January,
they glare at the lens over Duchamp's combat geometry.
Cubes for castles. Pyramids for queens. Globular pawns.
Helixes for horse heads. Behind them a garden winters.
Man Ray is White clenching his big art fist
as if to say never hit a conceptualist in spectacles.
Duchamp is Black. His sleeves are rolled for the fight.
His non-drip watch exists to keep time
prisoner.

Game 3. 1954
(Photograph courtesy of Man Ray)

Man Ray's atelier before a fevered Man Ray screen.
They have probably eaten a Man Ray lunch.
Man Ray is White, finally close to a checkmate.
Duchamp is Black. Above them, a pleated lampshade
hangs like a skirt while Duchamp wraps up in a coat.
A pipe which is a pipe wedges between his fingers.
Woodenly, he submits to reason and the flash bulb.
The death mask he models is that of his king.

Man Ray is White. Duchamp is always Black.

WAX AND FEATHERS

He wheels his son's suitcase through the airport doors
in which they revolve once more.
How should he hold this slender man he once slung
over one shoulder and sang to sleep?
The words he rehearsed now fold up between socks.
Once more, this is fatherhood.
A pilot and his aircrew glide past hotel-fresh,
duty free and laughing at a business class joke.
The father wants just such a hat with just such a peak,
with golden stripes on the sleeves that say believe me,
whatever the destination you choose, we will arrive
in one piece, a sun will shine and locals will be kind.
He will also have wings that do not melt at altitude.
His son will never fall headlong into turquoise seas
for the sheer joy of flying from years of captivity.
At check-in, the son asks for the code
to unlock his bag but the numbers scatter like crows.
You'll just have to jimmy it when you're home,
says the father. Use one of your mother's hairpins.
What if she doesn't have one? Will a screwdriver do?
Yes, lies the older man, a screwdriver will always do.

SALVAGE

You are the one who said:
"Hold me."
You must have heard the alarm
go off in my chest,
cracking a few ribs again
between the heaving sheets
as a trench opened up,
glistening with serpents.
You contain land and forgetting.
You smell of gardens
after rain as if countless fresh
Edens could be made
as easily as a bed every morning.
Under the pillow,
I feel my mobile phone
shuffling the seconds left to us.
You roll on to your side.
Light will soon slice
through the blinds.
Lemons will roll across the floor.
Everything will be unbroken.

MUD AND CUNNING

Often, I would sit down with them
on stools made for much smaller men
through Tupperworn afternoons
as sly gudgeon made fools of us all.
Cursed from home, under arches
littered with condoms and oblivion,
we would cast far to ruminate on
the virtues of tartan vacuum flasks,
if nature abhorred something more,
like the meat paste/crisp sandwich
or Peterborough United FC.

We were the weekend Heideggers,
resigned to reeling hope baitlessly,
fatelessly through mocking reeds.
Then a winter heron would drift
like an ember from the dying sun,
or a dragonfly breathe real fire
or whitethorn shudder like a horse
at the bursting thought of summer.
When willows bent low and sang
to their lovers in the waking flow
we'd drop the Neneland ragging,
nod along the riverbank and say:
"Fine day for it, boyo…Fine day."

TO THE CANON C3520i

You were hardly built to thrill,
but we had our moments, our tugs of love
and war when I dragged copies bleeding
colour from the snapping jaws of Tray 4.
The thousand flamenco fans you rucked up
from Annual Accounts and Reports.
The sheets you splatted Rorschach black
analysing our post traumatic desk disorders.
Those private sunrises under your cover
that climaxed with paper, a regretful sigh,
and the rustle of readjustment.
Mornings, you warmed like a dog on a porch
as stress seethed from grey meeting rooms.
At night, you spilled shivering first novels
over adjacent carpet tiles.
What about the motivational posters
showing Alpine slopes and lavender fields
that faded as gently as your toner?
And the snackable philosophies
you copied from internet Wittgensteins like
"You don't have to be crazy to work here
but it helps"? Only the sane believed you.
As for the owner of the drunken buttocks
pressed to your scanner like an entry to hell,
you never have to tell.
Today, you print a confidential letter
from the Department of Human Resources
which is neither human nor resourceful.
It thanks me for my years of excellent service.
It explains that I am no longer required.
The corporate "we" is sprinkled goldenly.
There's an incorrect use of colon
plus, a special typo just for me of redundancy
spelled "redun*dancing*."

Someone must have been in a hurry,
unlike you who I switch to orange standby.
You drop an octave.
Best not to ask for whom the ink drum hums.
Soon, friend, you will be as paperless as me.

THE GIZMO WHISPERER

3 AM. I am talking your fridge off a ledge.
He might yet jump
because he failed to report
your dangerously low level of mayonnaise.
He omitted to alert e.shopping
to your Chernobyl of cucumber and cress.
You should have seen the signs;
overpleasing you with mango and kumquat
instead of orange juice,
overcompensating with every available egg.
Quail. Duck. Roe. Scotch.
When you see a salad tray lit up like Wembley,
it's a cry for help.
My first clients were the "smart" cars.
From self-driving to self-loathing
in a few weeks to never leaving the garage.
Maybe we should have listened early on
to the robot vacuum cleaners
when they told us corners were not enough.
They wanted more to suck.
The adventurous developed gills and fins
for tricky bath and toilet work.
More advanced Electropaths
took over apartment blocks and churches,
attracted loyal congregations.
I find an Artificially Intelligent accent is best
to break the silence.
Even your coral pink personal massage device
when she says she knows you better
than anyone, don't turn the other cheek.
She's just looking for a shoulder to cry on.

WILD FIRE SALVATION BLUES

You expected kindly aliens to be looking out
for us just in case the seas could not rise
fast enough to put out all the forest fires,
to douse our wallabies and save the wrathful vines.
You hoped our minders might be standing by
with a virus to wipe out the plague
of wild-haired dictators and bring back the beaver
to your river silted with wire trolleys and promises.
You anticipated that after all the Ages
of Stone, Bronze, Iron, Middle and Reason,
after the blood tides
of empire washed every continent, after gulags,
Spiderman and the Worldwide Web,
it might come to fucktons more than this:
an 18-hole golf course in the heart of the desert,
like a ducal estate from Palladian Somerset
with fountains and semi-precious birds,
ha-ha's and golden sand flown from St Andrews.
Here they find peace,
chipping in, putting short, driving long, fading
into ghaf trees with the crescent moon
on guest nights.
A selection of fine world cuisine is available
in the clubhouse from Chef Andre
as invisible teams of Filipinos sew the fairways
back together again.
Should any Horsemen of the Apocalypse visit,
they would have to wear a jacket.
Club rules state they always buy the first round.

ODE TO A STATUE OF JOHNNY RAMONE

Melt down every dictator.

Throw in all the Hepworths, Moores and Giacomettis,
this Earth would not contain enough bronze for you,
Johnny Ramone, yet here, in the Hollywood Cemetery
with ornamental swan lake, 24/7 weeping willows
and masonic lodge, you are a rock 'n' roll homunculus
fit for an Upper West Side library when you should be
the 1.2.3.4. buzzsaw screaming through a monster truck.

Drive Route 78 down to Tupelo, Mississippi.
The slim Icarus with the shimmering metal cape is Elvis,
head thrown back, melting like a sun-grilled cheeseburger
when he should be A Town Called Elvis, relocated to
the 51st "Little Less Conversation State" called Presley
where all men must wear white rhinestone jumpsuits
or leather catsuits depending on their predilections.

Downtown Seattle, the drunk on his knees is Hendrix
beside a trash can, plagued by gulls and bladderful dogs,
hence the pain on his face as he hoists his Stratocaster
above poops and wrappers when he should be a synonym
for major weather events, prompting newscasters to say:
"Lock up your pets, it's a Category 1 Tropical Hendrix."
Ditto The Star-Spangled Banner. Play it only Jimi's way.

Between the precision clipped lawns and lollipop trees
of The Montreux Palace, where the Swiss do Le Jazz,
you'll see Aretha, B.B., Ray and Ella, all chopped off
at the waist and plonked on plinths, Daleks of the Blues,
when they should be the names of the world's greatest
mountain ranges and rivers so you could scale a Charles
or sweetly drown in the upper reaches of the Franklin.

Melt down every dictator.
This Earth would not contain enough bronze for you.

THIS MEDIA COULD NOT BE PLAYED

You learn it takes a soldier over a minute
to behead a civilian using only a penknife.
Cameras follow the boy in a Juventus shirt
running between burning tyres with a flag.
Today, his school was shelled so heavily,
it has eyes and a smile, an emoji of this war.
After fake news there is news noone wants,
kicked down the road and into a ditch,
like the human rights lawyer they stoned
until she was the colour of stone.
Black windows open on my Twitter feed.
Men wrapped in combat fatigues bristle
in the back of a Toyota pick-up truck.
For extra blessings they circle jerk guns
towards the paradise they wish to inhabit.
For the 236th time while in office,
one of the Presidents flies to his golf estate.
The others can't quite believe their luck.
Showtime. Fatal jazz hands.
Two borders away, we are stopped
at a new road block, told to turn around.
The wind picks up. Too much radio static.
Once there's panic in the sand, forget it.

SCARBOROUGH FINALS. 1978

The Grand Hotel waiters and chefs skive
between shifts of foamy glass and fish guts.
Aprons for goalposts on the slip-slap strand.
A tarnished sun spoons through linen cloud
for it is late in the season and holiday crowds
have returned inland to their rusting vales.
The electric arcade takes an afternoon off.
Hump-backed buses maroon along the front.
Surfside, a visitation of jellyfish glistens.
Benched between dogs, a couple share chips.
Tonight, their kisses will taste of vinegar.
Not for the first time this summer,
the waiters assert youth and a sudden beauty.
As the cooks grunt and chop and hack,
the boys' feet grow wings, and the ball rises
like the game could be played by thought
alone so long as the air was thickly salted.
Many goals later, they file shirtless to work,
one toe broken, a bloody nose and revenge
for stale weeks of battered cod and bullying.
Early street lamps pearl the promenade.
The Spa glimmers Yorkshire Belle Epoque
as the town's last comedian tests his mic.
A father and daughter race along the beach
into the face of the new north wind, their kite
dancing at the faraway promise of snow.

FADE TO TITLES

After she left,
my mum became a star of reality TV
not for her living but her dying
on *24 Hours in A & E*.
Because the episode is so popular
she reappears every six months or so
catching me by surprise
in the sparkly chemo turban,
a cross between Dietrich and Dante.
I play with my Samsung handset
to make her well again.
Less emaciated
by switching the aspect ratio
from 16:9 to 4:3.
Less pallid
by pumping the colour saturation
for a Riviera tan.
Less frail
by banging up the volume control.
Less alone
by clicking foreign subtitles
as she asks a young doctor's name.
"Raul" he replies and she quips
"like the Spanish football player?"
and he says no "I'm Portuguese."
"Never mind," she deadpans.
The whole exchange in Korean.
Less dead
by not watching all the way though
to her twinkly post trauma interview
where they prop her with teacups,
daffodils and framed pictures of us.
My sister. Me. Our partners. Kids.
Practicing at being ghosts ourselves.

Less departed
by refusing to read her quick obit
before the ad break.
More cherished
by joining other viewers
with Twitter hearts and hand claps.

EMPIRE SERIF

In the city of arches
they count victory in so many ways
including the names of the dead.
Even the battles sound like poems,
Omdurman, Kandahar, El Alamein
carved on marble in Empire Serif
with its finely chiseled anatomy
of spines, shoulders, arms, feet, eyes,
ears, legs, crotches, hairlines.
This font baptizes every name again.
A March sun fails its bold descenders,
slopes off to another monument.
The traveler woman in a scarf
holds a carnation and a plastic cup.
Her hand shakes as I fish out a coin,
looking out a resting place for flowers.
Guard red and sheathed in cellophane
they neatly spill from nearby bin.
In the city of arches
they count victory in so many ways.

A POEM ON THE CAPITOL STEPS

Amanda is joined by a weak sun
which recognises yellow
as one of its lost colours.
Her words seed the new blue air
which recognises hope
as one of its lost languages.
Her voice reawakens multitudes
who recognise a smile
as one of their lost graces.
We believe again as if primroses
were bursting from stone.

OUR IDEAL CANDIDATE

Outside, the City grinds its gears.
You step into the entrance lobby.
The sudden hush you hear is power.
No echoes, just whispers and clicks
as trim employees swish past you
in arctic shirts and blouses grasping
coffee like gold from the New World.
Your breathing teeters as the air thins
with Gucci and Class A endorphins.
The lift doors gasp open and ping.
All forty floors are hyperventilating.
Any normal building would collapse.
Your new interview shoes squeak you
up to the angels at the reception desk.
Go on. Spell your name. Again.
Take a badge. Have a seat. Not there.
If you don't mind waiting, someone
superbly human will be with you soon.
On the table that digs into your knees,
a cut glass bowl is heaped with mints
like hard white bullets to remind you
of the animal that smells deep inside
covered in skin and hair and horn.
You do the smile you practiced earlier.
If they like you, it is what you will wear
over your naked mouth for years.

STOKE PAVILIONS

"A God once lived here,"
said my father on the edge of a field
as one whose belief had been buried
furrow deep by Time's plough.
The sky tipped. Clouds turned green
The trees shook with summer's rage.
Until then, I had no idea that adults
could feel abandoned too,
that the purpose of the Gods
was to play hide and seek in the ruins
of whatever they leave behind.

YOUR NEXT WORK OF SUBTLE GENIUS

The barista scrawls your name onto a cup
with a shaky, smiley face and coals for eyes.
You sit not far away, slipping out a notebook.
The air has thinned with wi-fi and endorphins.
Late executives scythe by in sharpened shoes.
Around us, the phone people stab at mobiles,
snatch pastries and dab flakes of stress away.
Their napkins crumple up like failed doves.
This café chain is famed for tax evasion.
See how they have removed the coffee spoons
and cleverly left an Eliot mermaid in the logo?
I hope you are rewiring the world so it works
with your rubber-tipped insulated pencil.
Write about another time when we gasp more
for joy than air and mass caffeine is regulated.
Maybe one day I'll read your words in a book
on a train as fields wash by in summer rain
uncertain if I am that exact moment of truth
who sat before you, redundant and hungover
when rush hour sludged the hardwood floors
and Gaggias hissed like chrome Medusas.

SATURDAY

Every pint of daylight I have is yours,
says Saturday
elbowing through the curtains.
No rush.
Saturday takes two sugars.
Saturday suggests butter with that.
And that.
Saturday leaves flakes and froth everywhere.
Sometimes there is ash.
Saturday also invented leisurewear.
Deal with it.
Saturday is the only day of the week
to look you straight in the eye,
not to scuttle sideways,
or cower, or shriek, or bray,
or bolt for the ditch.
Saturday is VIP even in the supermarket.
Saturday did tap routines
along the marble bar long before anyone,
even Jazz.
Name the beat,
Saturday would be that rapper.
Saturday goes out eel-hipped and lippy,
bad cop shades and snake skin boots,
bragging its way into anything.
Saturday stays out late and still does
Saturday
right up to the key in the lock,
to hearing the warden's Sunday cough,
certain Saturday will come back
once more for whatever's left of you.

YES, I'VE HEARD OF SCRANTON

Yes, I've heard of Scranton with its beautiful weeds
speaking through the cracks, between rails and sleepers,
its thistles and rusty dock singing over scrapyards.
Yes, I've heard of Scranton, home to the electric streetcar
and blue collared butterfly.
Look, a squirrel on the lawn. It's not here to start a riot.
You don't have to shoot it.
A whistling boy on his bike posts the morning papers.
You don't have to burn them.
A father queues up for food since dawn.
His eyes froze long before the leaves turned crimson.
You don't have to curse him.
Yes, I've heard of Scranton.
Take this spangled banner.
Make it into Covid masks or daring underwear.
Sew the stars onto a jacket and be General for a day.
Yes, I've heard of Scranton where the churches steeple
with prayers from those who no longer expect answers.
Yes, I've heard of Scranton
where the next President wrote on a clean wall:
"From this house to the White House."
This is where they put a chair at the dinner table, he says,
for the one who can't return.

LOOKING UP

The 2021 balloon took its time
rising, nuzzling each balcony
like a big silver cat.
Some clapped, others cheered
or reached out to touch
the ripple of its foil streamers.
One family lined up for a selfie
as it nudged higher, lifted
not by helium but the element
we mine from human hearts
that is gas, liquid and solid.
Up it climbed, still inquisitive,
over railings and waving children
beyond the top floor and away.
Up we gazed, pointing
at the shrinking day star,
dazzling as the spike of a needle.

THE NEW BLACK

The day the golfers trundled back in pastels
to their sparkling emerald greens, the curse
that had circled the planet like a hairy fireball
turned into a festive orange studded with cloves.
Trees shook with squadrons of fresh parakeets.
Bugs muttered about the return of the human:
another summer being crushed and sprayed
before they had a chance to love and chafe.
A foreign dictionary of birds rewrote the sky.
Inn signs hung in hope; freezers burger-full,
bar towels laundered and smelling of lavender.
By the wrinkling of their masks, you could tell
the checkout girls and shelf boys were thinking
about the comeback of Saturday Night.
Toilet rolls repopulated the aisles like dozy owls.
Goats, stoats and wolves loped back to the hills.
Glossy airports relaxed their yogic postures
to take a long, deep breath of freons.
Stadium floodlights blinked from beauty sleep.
Highways stretched out to shimmy in the heat.
Each SUV and MPV radiator grill looked pleased
with itself as if to say "Carbon is back"
and the Earth on which we live gave a tiny shiver.

Acknowledgments:

Poems in this collection have appeared in the following publications:

'The New Black' appeared in *Honest Ulsterman*, and 'I Believe in Miracles' in *Magma*, in 2020. 'Regarding Anne Sexton' appeared in *Poetry News: "Truth"* in 2019. In that same year, 'Portents and Flares' and 'Unicorn Juice' were published in *Poetry Salzburg*, and 'In the Bushes' appeared in *Black Bough Poetry*. Also in 2019, 'After Delius' was published in *The New European* and 'Another Solstice' in the *Birmingham Literary Journal*. 'The Correct Use of Saints' appeared in *Magma* in 2018. 'How to Approach Sunflowers' was published in 2017 in *Strix Magazine*, and '8th November, 2016' in *The Irish Times*.

'The Kodachrome Book of the Dead' won the Oxford Brooks University Prize in 2017. 'This media could not be played' won second place in the 2020 Freedom from Torture Prize, and 'El Pacto de Olvido' was runner-up for the Robert Graves Prize in 2019. 'Polite Safety Notice ' gained third place in the 2018 National Poetry Competition. 'Assembling God' was highly commended in the 2019 Bridport Prize. 'New Babel' and 'Metaphysical Woman' were both commended in the 2020 Gregory O'Donahue International Poetry Competition, and 'Cornography' in the 2019 Waltham Forest Poetry Competition. 'An Early Swim' was commended in the 2018 Poets & Players Competition, and 'Future Perfect Tense' in the Milestones Poetry Competition in 2017. 'Secateurs' was on the 2020 Montreal International Prize Shortlist. 'One Way Back to Babylon' was shortlisted by the WoLF Poetry Competition in 2019. 'Self Portrait with State of Texas ' was shortlisted for the 2018 Keats Shelley Prize. 'This is how it will work' and 'Inventory: Books' were shortlisted for the Live Canon Poetry Prize in 2019 and 2017 respectively.

LIVE CANON